Woodpeckers

by Stan Tekiela

Adventure Publications
Cambridge, Minnesota

Dedication

To Kathy, for being so special to me.

Acknowledgments

Thanks to the Bird Collection, Bell Museum of Natural History, University of Minnesota (St. Paul) and the All Seasons Wild Bird Stores in Minnesota, which have been instrumental in obtaining the seed images in this book.

Thanks also to Jim and Carol Zipp, good friends and bird store owners, for reviewing this book.

Credits

Cover photos of birds by Stan Tekiela

All photos by Stan Tekiela except pg. 10 (White-headed) by Paul Bannick and pg. 11 (Lewis's) by Rick and Nora Bowers. All full-page bird images and the image on pg. 37 are Downy Woodpeckers unless otherwise labeled.

Edited by Sandy Livoti

Cover and book design by Jonathan Norberg

10 9 8 7 6 5 4 3 2 1

Copyright 2017 by Stan Tekiela
Published by Adventure Publications
An imprint of AdventureKEEN
820 Cleveland Street South
Cambridge, Minnesota 55008
(800) 678-7006
www.adventurepublications.net
All rights reserved
Printed in China
ISBN: 978-1-59193-707-4; eISBN: 978-1-59393-733-3

Table of Contents

All About Woodpeckers

I believe that woodpeckers are some of the most extraordinary birds on the planet. For example, they land vertically on the sides of trees as if gravity didn't exist. This sets them apart from other birds, which land on horizontal branches and other objects with the aid of gravity. Combine that with the amazing capability to excavate holes in very hard wood with just their beaks, and you've got some extremely remarkable birds!

Woodpeckers have wonderful markings and colors. Not only that, nearly all woodpecker species have marks that distinguish the males from the females. Many woodpeckers have a small red, yellow or black mark on or near the head that indicates the bird is a male.

Woodpeckers, which include sapsuckers and flickers, are in the Picidae family—a very different group from our backyard perching birds. There are about 200 woodpecker species in the world, with 22 in the United States and Canada. The most common species by far is the Downy Woodpecker, which resides in all U.S. states and much of Canada year-round.

Nearly all woodpeckers are primary cavity nesters, meaning they excavate their own cavities. House Wrens, bluebirds and all other cavity nesters move into these cavities after the woodpeckers have left. This makes the woodpecker's excavation activity extremely important.

Facts

Relative Size: the Downy Woodpecker is about half the size of an American Robin

Length: 5.5–6.5" (14–16 cm)

Wingspan: 10–12" (25–30 cm)

Weight: .75–1 oz. (21–28 g)

Male: red mark on the back of head and white stripe down the back, black-and-white spotted wings, all-white belly, white tail with small black spots on the sides, black line through each eye, short black bill

Female: same as male except it lacks the red mark on head

Juvenile: same as female, some have a red mark near the forehead

Nest: cavity; 4–5" (10–13 cm) in diameter, 2.5–3.5" (6–9 cm) high; male and female excavate

Migration: non-migrator

Food: insects, seeds; comes to seed and suet feeders

Range & Habitat

The Downy Woodpecker is the most common and one of the most widespread woodpeckers in the United States and Canada. Red-headed Woodpeckers used to be the most common and widespread woodpecker, but they aren't nearly as abundant anymore. Other species, such as Red-cockaded, Nuttall's and Arizona Woodpeckers, occur only in restricted regions.

Acorn Woodpeckers are some of the most amazing-looking woodpeckers! Sapsuckers are also a type of woodpecker. Four distinctive sapsucker species are spread across the United States.

Wooded backyards and yards with mature trees are excellent habitats for woodpeckers. Preserving some dead trees or branches goes a long way to provide nesting habitat for our woodpecker friends.

The maps on pages 9–11 represent the ranges of our 22 species of woodpeckers in the United States and Canada. They do not, however, reflect the density or population of the birds.

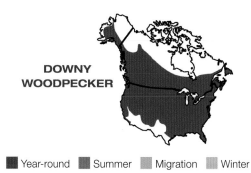

DOWNY WOODPECKER

■ Year-round ■ Summer ■ Migration ■ Winter

Woodpeckers are organized by size, smallest to largest.

■ Year-round ■ Summer ■ Migration ■ Winter

Ladder-backed Woodpecker

Nuttall's Woodpecker

Arizona Woodpecker

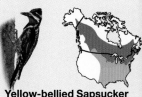

Yellow-bellied Sapsucker

Red-naped Sapsucker

Red-breasted Sapsucker

American Three-toed Woodpecker

White-headed Woodpecker

Red-cockaded Woodpecker

Hairy Woodpecker

Red-headed Woodpecker

Gila Woodpecker

Acorn Woodpecker

Williamson's Sapsucker

Red-bellied Woodpecker

Golden-fronted Woodpecker

Black-backed Woodpecker

Gilded Flicker

Northern Flicker

Lewis's Woodpecker

Pileated Woodpecker

11

Red-bellied Woodpecker

Calls & Drumming

Each woodpecker species has its own unique, primitive call. Most of these calls are sharp and often repeated over and over to attract a mate or guard a territory.

In addition, many woodpecker species drum loudly on hollow branches or logs, much like a percussionist on a drum. Drumming can be heard from great distances.

Woodpeckers call and drum from March through June. At this time they are establishing their home range and attracting a mate, followed by nesting. By midsummer they stop defending territory and fall silent as they busily raise their young.

To keep in contact without having to look, males and females give short, soft, metallic-sounding call notes. When they are upset, they give loud threat or distress calls—a staccato call of notes—while spreading their wings and tail feathers to look large and menacing.

QUICK-TIPS

- Downy Woodpeckers call a rapid "peek-peek-peek"
- The calls of Downies last about 2 seconds and descend in pitch toward the end
- Woodpeckers drum about 20 strikes per second
- Drumming activity rarely causes any damage to the object of the drumming
- Except for sapsuckers, which have irregular drumming, all woodpeckers have regular, steady drumming
- Drumming can be unique to each species and is a good way to help identify the drummer

Pileated Woodpecker

Cavity Nests

All of our woodpeckers construct similar cavity nests in trees. Some, such as Northern Flickers, occasionally use natural tree cavities. Most excavate and use the cavity only once to raise their young. However, the Pileated Woodpecker sometimes uses its cavity for several consecutive years or returns to an old cavity after many years absent. The Red-headed Woodpecker often uses its cavity all year long for many years.

Cavities can be 6–60 feet above the ground. Most are excavated in dead trees. Smaller woodpeckers, such as Downies, often build lower in trees. A Downy entrance is a round hole, 1½ inches across. The cavity is about 6–12 inches deep and slightly wider at the bottom.

After excavating, woodpeckers do not bring in any nesting material. Females lay eggs on the bed of wood chips at the cavity bottom. The cavity interior provides a stable microclimate for the eggs and developing chicks and protects against predators and inclement weather.

Both parents excavate, but not together. After much chiseling, the parent enters the hole and collects a mouthful of chips. Poking its head out of the hole, the bird spits out the chips and shakes its head to clear away the dust and debris on its beak.

Most construction occurs early in the morning. Often the parents work on the cavity daily, but only for a short time. Usually it takes 13–16 days to complete a cavity nest, depending on the hardness of the wood.

Eggs, Chicks & Juveniles

Downy Woodpeckers usually raise just one brood per season. The male establishes a territory in March and April, and the female chooses the cavity site and begins construction in April and May. Females lay upwards of 5–6 pure white eggs. Camouflage markings aren't needed because the dark cavity hides the eggs.

At birth, chicks are naked, helpless and unable to regulate their own body temperature. The mother must continue to sit on them (brood) until they have enough feathers to keep warm, usually about 7 days. The male brings in most of the food for the chicks and the mother.

Within 20–25 days of hatching, the chicks are ready to leave the nest (fledge). By this time they are juveniles, nearly full size and look like the adults. They follow their parents around, fluttering their wings and squawking to beg for food. Adults land nearby to feed them.

Broods: 1 per season

Clutch Size: 3–6 eggs (4–5 average)

Egg Length: .8" (2 cm)

Egg Color: white with no markings

Incubation: 11–12 days; female incubates during the day, male at night

Hatchlings: naked except for sparse tufts of down feathers; eyes and ears are sealed shut

Fledging: 20–25 days

Northern Flicker

Woodpecker Trivia

- The Downy Woodpecker is the smallest woodpecker species in North America.

- Downy Woodpeckers are some of the first birds to discover a new bird feeder.

- Downies are often not afraid of people, allowing you to approach very closely before they take flight.

- The name "Downy" refers to the fluffy feathers and soft bristles that cover the bird.

- When drumming on hollow logs, Downies strike their bills about 16–20 times per second.

- Downies take several weeks to make a nest cavity, often excavating only about 30 minutes per day.

- Some young male Downy Woodpeckers have a red mark near their foreheads.

- Most Downies live only 4–6 years; however, the oldest one in the wild lived to reach 11 years and 5 months!

- Downy and Hairy Woodpeckers join other birds during winter to form a "winter flock" that moves around together to forage for food.

- The Pileated Woodpecker is the largest woodpecker species in the United States and Canada, but it is shy around people and will fly off if it sees you.

- All sapsucker and flicker species are woodpeckers.

- Sapsuckers don't actually suck sap; they drill holes in horizontal patterns in tree trunks and then lap up the sap. They also eat the insects that come to the sap.

- There are two varieties of Northern Flicker. In the eastern half of the country, flickers have yellow-shafted feathers. In western areas, the shafts are red.

- Flickers prefer ants and beetles and are the only woodpeckers to regularly feed on the ground.

- Woodpeckers are found in nearly all kinds of habitats, including deserts.

- Male woodpeckers tend to forage for food on thinner branches, shrubs and weed stems than their female counterparts, which prefer larger perches.

- Some woodpecker species stop at hummingbird feeders to enjoy a few sips of the sweet nectar.

- Woodpeckers are omnivores. Besides insects, tree sap and nectar, they also eat seeds, nuts, and even the yolk of other bird eggs.

- Woodpeckers have extremely long tongues—some of the longest in the bird world! Anchoring near the forehead, the tongue wraps around the outer surface of the skull and extends to the tip of the bill, where it exits the mouth.

- Most woodpecker species have two toes pointing forward and two pointing back (zygodactyl). Other birds have three toes pointing forward and only one pointing back.

- Woodpeckers have short, stout legs that keep their bodies close to trunks while clinging to trees.

- Woodpeckers have 10 very stiff tail feathers that act like the third leg of a tripod when they cling to trees.

- Woodpeckers peck wood about 8,000—12,000 times each day.

- Most woodpeckers are a combination of black and white with a splash of red. The next most common color is brown.

- Woodpeckers are not songbirds. They don't make musical notes or sing songs to attract a mate or defend a home range.

- Woodpeckers rarely, if ever, take a water bath.

- Woodpeckers have a distinctive undulating flight that consists of a number of rapid wing beats, causing a rise in flight, and tucking the wings and gliding, which produces descent.

- Most woodpecker species do not migrate. Remaining in an area often provides an early start for establishing a territory and choosing a mate in spring.

- Male woodpeckers do most of the egg incubation at night; the females incubate during the day.

- Woody Woodpecker was created by Walter Lantz Productions and storyboard artist Ben Hardaway in 1940. Woody was styled after the Acorn Woodpecker, although some think it was the Pileated Woodpecker that he really took after.

Hairy Woodpecker (left)
and Downy Woodpecker

Feeding Woodpeckers

Attracting woodpeckers is fairly easy when you offer choice foods at feeding stations. Suet and peanuts are the two best foods to get them to visit your yard.

Suet is fat rendered mainly from the kidneys and loins of cattle and sheep. Oftentimes suet is combined with bits of other food items and formed into solid cakes, which can be offered in wire or mesh cages. Suet cages allow the birds to reach the food with their bills, but they can't take the entire cake. Another great way to appeal to woodpeckers is to drill good-sized holes into a log and stuff them with round suet plugs.

Suet is also sold raw at your local butcher shop or meat market and usually comes in an onion or mesh bag. Simply hang this from a shepherd's hook and let the birds have at it. During deer hunting season or after a cow slaughter, put out a rib cage in your backyard to draw in more woodpeckers.

Suet is a real fat product that melts, drips and spoils in warm temperatures, so most people offer it just in winter. However, there are no-melt suet cakes that will withstand warmer weather. They contain more plant material but still provide the nutrition that woodpeckers need. Many no-melt varieties come with seeds, fruit and insects embedded and are a great way to feed woodpeckers all year long.

Another surefire way to get woodpeckers to come to your feeding station is to offer peanuts. You can put out peanuts in any season and enjoy woodpeckers in your yard year-round. Peanuts can be offered in different ways, and each one is as good as the next.

Whole peanuts in the shell can be encased in wire mesh feeders. These openings are large enough for the birds to pull out one shell with peanuts at a time.

Peanuts out of the shell are known across the bird feeding industry as peanut hearts, pieces or pick-outs. Feeders for pick-outs have smaller openings that allow woodpeckers to extract just one shelled nut at a time. Offering peanut hearts is one of the best ways to feed woodpeckers. All woodpecker species in your area will come to these feeders and enjoy the treat.

In addition to peanuts, many woodpecker species also love peanut butter. It's high in protein and oil but can be messy for both you and the birds, even in specialized feeders. Consider spreading small amounts on tree bark or suet cakes.

Standard seed feeders attract woodpeckers as well as other birds. Black oil sunflower seed is the best kind of birdseed to offer. Woodpeckers will gather a few seeds and crack them open under the cover of tree branches.

Woodpeckers also feed on mealworms in feeders. Offer small containers of live or dried mealworms to provide insect protein early in spring before bugs are plentiful or later in fall after a hard frost.

Suet

Suet: One of the best ways to attract woodpeckers is with suet. Suet cakes are made mainly from fat around the loins and kidneys of cows and sheep, although more and more suet is coming from fat anywhere on the animals.

Suet is an extremely high-energy food with a high calorie count, and woodpeckers easily digest it. Cakes are often mixed with cracked corn, seeds, insects, nuts, dried fruit or a combination of these foods. Offering different varieties of suet is a great way to give your woodpeckers especially tasty treats.

Offer suet in wire feeders with a bottom perch. These allow woodpeckers to get to the cake and break off a small piece. Hang feeders from poles or fasten to posts. Protect these feeders from squirrels, raccoons, chipmunks and opossums, which will take the entire cake.

Peanuts & Peanut Butter

Peanuts: Peanuts are another excellent option to feed woodpeckers. The peanut plant (*Arachis hypogaea*) is a member of the legume or bean family and grows underground. With 45 percent fat and 24 percent protein, peanuts are also a good source of vitamins A and E, as well as zinc, iron and potassium.

Woodpeckers eat peanuts in any form—whole in the shell, shelled, or in small chips. Peanut pieces or pick-outs are popular in seed mixes and suet. Birds gobble these quickly, so sprinkle them with birdseed or place them in a feeder with a tight mesh covering to prevent large amounts from spilling out all at once.

Try offering peanuts in the shell to your woodpeckers. Use a metal mesh feeder with large openings, and soon the birds will be pulling out entire nuts. Peanuts get wet and will mold, so don't put out a lot at one time.

Smooth or chunky peanut butter is another good food to attract wood-peckers to your yard. Offer it like suet in specialized feeders or just smear it on a chunk of bark directly on a tree or on a cake of suet. You can offer this high-energy food in your own creative ways. However you present it, the woodpeckers will quickly find it.

Seeds & Grains

Black Oil Sunflower: Studies have shown that woodpeckers prefer black oil sunflower seeds above all other commercial birdseed. Black oilers are smooth black seeds from the common sunflower plant, *Helianthus annuus*.

Woodpeckers have no trouble cracking open these seeds with their large, strong bills.

Black oilers contain more fat in the form of oil than other seeds, hence the name. They are meatier and pack more nourishment per bite than just about any other bird food on the market. These sunflower seeds have a nutritional value of 28 percent fat, 15 percent protein and 25 percent fiber, and they supply vitamins B and E, as well as calcium, iron and potassium.

Striped Sunflower: These sunflower seeds have a thin white stripe. Larger than black oil sunflower seeds, they have a thicker hull, making them harder to split. Nevertheless, woodpeckers open them easily and like them a lot. Sometimes called stripers, people also enjoy these seeds, which are high in fat, protein, vitamins and fiber.

Hulled Sunflower: Hulled sunflower is just the meat or nutmeat of the sunflower seed without the hard, inedible outer shell. The nutritional content is the same as black oil and striped sunflower seeds. There is no possibility for these seeds to germinate, so the bags are marketed as non-germinating or no-mess mixes. With hulled sunflower, you won't need to rake up or blow away discarded hulls under your feeders.

Hulled sunflower is sold as whole nuts, or pieces and chips. The expense of shelling makes this feed more expensive, but the benefits outweigh the cost. Most birdseed is sold by weight, and with hulled sunflower you're not paying for the inedible shells.

Cracked Corn: At a wonderful low cost, cracked corn is a great option to feed many woodpeckers on the ground. Corn will also attract rabbits, squirrels, raccoons, opossums, and other birds. Cracked corn offerings keep squirrels busy with something to eat, leaving your feeders with the higher priced foods for the woodpeckers.

Cracked corn is just what it sounds like—dried whole corn kernels that have been cracked. There can be lots of dust associated with cracked corn, but it's worth it. This food won't sprout and grow in your garden or lawn, and birds eat all the kernels, so there's no waste. Low in fat but high in protein and fiber, it is often a base in bird food blends. Offer it in large open-tray, fly-through or ground feeders, or sprinkle it directly on the ground.

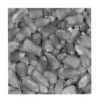

Whole Corn: Whole corn consists of entire kernels of dried corn and is often part of the base of wild bird food mixes. It is slightly more desirable to woodpeckers than cracked corn and usually is thought of as wildlife food because it attracts squirrels, chipmunks, raccoons, opossums and other animals. Offer it in a large tray or a trough ground feeder, or simply spread it on the ground.

Live & Dried Mealworms

Mealworms: Mealworms are the worm-like larvae of darkling beetles, which are flightless insects. A great source of protein, calcium and vitamins, live or dried mealworms attract woodpeckers as well as a variety of birds that don't normally come to traditional seed feeders. Both mealworm offerings are sold in large quantities, and for good reason. When woodpeckers find them, they gorge themselves. Live mealworms (top) must be stored in a container from which they cannot escape. A steep container with slippery sides is essential and should be refrigerated. Offer dried mealworms (bottom) in a shallow tray.

Fresh & Dried Fruits

Fruits: Many fresh fruits, such as bananas, apples, melons and grapes, as well as dried fruits, like raisins, currants, dates and prunes, are good choices to offer woodpeckers.

Some woodpeckers come to orange halves sunny-side up and secured with a nail. Fresh fruit can get messy and attract insects and animals, so put it on a platform with a squirrel or raccoon baffle as a deterrent. Add dried fruit to seed feeders. Pulling out dried fruit from any type of seed feeder is a great treat.

Storing Bird Food

Storing birdseed safely is easy. Keep it out of the house, preferably in a cool, dry place away from direct sunlight. Garages and sheds are the best places to stow feed, because the cooler temperatures there will reduce the number of grain moths hatching out of seeds.

Transfer seed out of its original plastic or paper bag into a clean container. The container should be upright, semi-airtight and be able to prevent mice, chipmunks and other rodents from chewing through and getting to the seed. Metal garbage cans are good choices for storage. Use several to store different kinds of food.

Try to avoid buying birdseed in very large quantities. Pick up just enough to feed woodpeckers and other birds for a month or so. Be sure to use up the oldest seed before opening your more recent purchases.

You can stock up on suet during the colder months of winter. In warmer months, store the cakes in a cold place where they won't melt.

Peanuts have high oil content and will spoil if purchased in such large quantities that they can't be used right away. Store bags of peanuts in cool-to-cold places and well-sealed containers to keep out any rodents.

Golden-fronted Woodpecker

Feeding Q&A

What's the best way to feed woodpeckers during summer?

By far the best way to feed woodpeckers in summer is with peanut pieces. There are a number of feeders that you can use to offer unshelled peanuts. You will find that many other bird species also enjoy this food.

Should I put out suet in summer months?

There are a number of no-melt suet products to feed woodpeckers during the warmer months. Offering suet year-round is a great way to keep woodpeckers around your yard to see and enjoy.

Live and dried mealworms—when is best?

Insect populations are not available during early spring and late fall, so live mealworms in a container or dried ones in a tray would be quickly devoured by the woodpeckers in your area. Whenever the weather is very cold, offer dried mealworms, because the live ones will stop moving and freeze before the birds can eat them.

What if I leave town or take a vacation?

It's not true that when you start feeding birds, you can't stop. Birds, including woodpeckers, do not become dependent on our feeders. They take advantage of the quick and easy offerings, but once those are gone they just fly off to another feeder or a wild food source. When you get back home, simply fill your feeders and watch the woodpeckers return. It won't take long.

Black oil and striped sunflower seeds—what's the difference?

Black oil sunflower seeds have around 70 percent nutmeat compared with just 57 percent in striped seeds. They also provide more calories than striped sunflower seeds in the form of fatty oils.

What should I do with old seeds?

Birdseed can go bad over time. If seeds smell bad, the oils have gone rancid and the batch needs to be thrown out. Grain moths, spiders and other pests can infest old birdseed. While bugs won't affect the overall seed, they may be trouble in the house. Wet seeds will spoil and stick together. The resulting mold or mildew can be fatal to birds, so discard seeds at the first sign of decay. Sprouted seeds are also red flags for disposal. Rodent infestation means urine or feces in the seed and you should not use it.

I have a birdbath. What about mosquitoes?

Birdbaths are essential for most backyard feeding stations, but mosquito proliferation is a concern. There are products that release a larvicide, killing all mosquito larvae, but a much more natural solution is to prevent them from developing at all. Moving the water with a small waterfall or battery-powered water wiggler does this, or simply change the water. It takes about seven days for mosquito larvae to develop, so use your garden hose or a bucket once a week to keep them in check.

Red-bellied Woodpecker

Bird Feeders

Offering assorted foods in feeders is sure to attract more woodpeckers and keep them coming back. For suet, a sturdy wire cage works well for woodpeckers. Suet cages often hang from a metal chain, or they can be fastened to existing feeders.

Tail-prop suet feeders are wonderful because they are designed to fit the unusually long body shape of a woodpecker and, more importantly, they give the bird a place to brace its tail while feeding on the suet.

Cling-to suet feeders have wire mesh on the underside, allowing woodpeckers to cling and feed. Birds with weaker feet can't eat the suet from these feeders.

Log feeders are small sections of logs with drilled holes evenly spaced around the entire log. Simply push suet plugs (available commercially) into the holes. At log

QUICK-TIPS

- Suet is great food to offer in winter, and no-melt suet is perfect for warmer weather feeding
- To make a log feeder, cut a section of a tree branch or trunk, drill 1¼–1½" holes in it and fill with suet
- The most versatile and favorite feeders of woodpeckers are metal tube feeders offering peanut hearts
- Choose platform feeders with a roof to help keep snow and rain from covering and soaking the seeds
- Tube feeders with a base for spilled or extra seeds give woodpeckers a place to perch while feeding

feeders, woodpeckers most closely replicate natural feeding behavior, and they love the easy source of food.

A wire tube peanut feeder is one of the best ways to attract woodpeckers. The small openings in the metal mesh allow just one peanut heart to be extracted at a time. These feeders come in a wide variety of shapes, from standard tubes, rings or circles, to square-sided tubes, to acorn-shaped styles with plastic sides.

Feeders with larger openings offer peanuts in the shell (whole peanuts). These feeders are popular with many woodpeckers and are quickly emptied. It's fun to watch them carry off their prize after working to remove it from the feeder.

When you offer seeds for woodpeckers, choose a feeder with a large platform (tray) and lots of headroom. These feeders allow woodpeckers to see the area in all directions and spot a predator approaching.

Larger hopper feeders with large places to land and feed are also a good choice. They don't need refilling as often as tray feeders, which hold just thin layers of seed.

Woodpeckers readily come to tube feeders for black oil sunflower seeds and other kinds of seeds.

Woodpeckers also enjoy mealworms, either live or dried, especially during the non-nesting season. Offering mealworms in a small plastic container with drilled holes for drainage works best.

You can make a mealworm tub feeder using a standard food storage container or old margarine tub. Be sure that the container does not allow the live mealworms to crawl out and that it has drainage holes in the bottom.

Feeder Types

Suet Feeder: A treated metal cage that holds a preformed cake of suet. Woodpeckers feed easily from styles with a tail prop, or with perching stands at the bottom. Some varieties have a roof, which sheds rainwater and snow accumulation and protects the food from bird scat. Hangs from a chain or pole, or attaches to a post.

Mesh Feeder: Constructed with metal mesh to hold peanuts. Usually consists of a long tube large enough to hold a plentiful supply of nuts. Can have small openings for peanut pieces or larger openings for peanuts in shells. Either way, woodpeckers need to work at getting the peanuts out. Releases only one nut at a time.

Platform, Tray or Ground Feeder: Also known as a fly-through feeder. Usually has a flat, open surface for seeds. Hangs from a series of wires or chains, rests on a central post or pole, or sits on the ground with the bottom of the tray about 12 inches off the ground. Made of wood or metal and often has a series of holes or slots for water drainage. Some have a protective roof.

Hopper Feeder: Often made of wood or recycled material. The central storage area, called the hopper, releases seeds slowly. A hopper holds many more seeds than other types of feeders and also keeps the food dry. You can see the seed level through the plexiglass sides, so you know when to refill.

Tube Feeder: A clear plastic tube with feeding pegs at metal openings for accessing seeds. Small to large sizes hold different amounts of seeds. Some varieties have a bottom tray for extra seeds, which woodpeckers use as a landing platform. Hang from shepherd's hooks or set on top of posts or poles.

Mealworm Feeder: These feeders are usually plastic with tall sides. The material needs to be slippery so live mealworms can't crawl out. Many kinds of dishes and trays can be used to offer mealworms to woodpeckers. You can recycle a plastic food container and fashion your own design. Just be sure to put some drainage holes in the bottom.

Placing Feeders

It's a distinct pleasure to see and feed woodpeckers, so always put feeders where you can easily watch and enjoy these amazing birds. They should be placed near an area where you spend a lot of time comfortably in your home and where you can see outside clearly.

Most feeding stations are about 20–40 feet away from residences. Placing feeders nearer will draw the birds to where you can easily see them. However, the closer the feeders, the more likely you will have window strikes.

Feeders close to shrubs or other cover give woodpeckers a place to stage and look for predators before flying in to feed. Plant cover also gives them a quick place to hide in case a hawk swoops in to snatch a feeder bird. Feeders in the middle of large open spaces usually will not attract many woodpeckers.

Place feeders where squirrels can't get to them. The basic placement rule is 5 feet and 8 feet—meaning that feeders should be at least 5 feet off the ground and at least 8 feet from any other surface from which a squirrel can jump. This includes trees, houses, sheds, charcoal grills, birdbaths, patio furniture and anything else a squirrel can climb to jump onto feeders.

When placing feeders, be sure to install a squirrel or raccoon baffle on each one. Baffles are metal tubes or flared metal shields that prevent animals from climbing your shepherd's hooks and accessing the bird food.

Choose a place where seed waste won't kill the grass. Perhaps landscape an area of the yard dedicated to bird feeding with rocks, shrubs and a water element.

More feeders bring in larger numbers of woodpeckers. Provide a variety of feeders to attract more birds. If possible, choose one of each type to offer a nutritious, well-balanced assortment of food.

Acorn Woodpecker

Maintaining Feeders & Good Practices

Feeder maintenance is essential for the overall health of woodpeckers. How often you clean your feeders depends on the weather and season. Cleaning is more important during summer than winter, and feeders in wet environments require more cleaning than those in dry climates. Bird feeders offering food with a high fat content, such as suet, need to be cleaned more often than those holding less fatty foods.

Bird feeders are the number one place where disease is spread among bird species. Dirty or contaminated feeders hold bacteria, mold and viruses that can sicken or kill the birds.

A number of transmissible diseases are associated with birds, including woodpeckers, and their droppings. To be safe, use good hygiene practices and take some basic precautions when filling or cleaning your feeders.

For example, when you clean the feeders, wear rubber gloves. After filling or cleaning feeders, vigorously wash your gloved hands and cleaning brushes with warm, soapy water. Use paper towels to pat dry, and discard the towels.

Cleaning Your Feeders

Always try to use rubber gloves when handling your feeders and cleaning the feeding area because there are several diseases that can be picked up from bird droppings. *Histoplasma capsulatum* is a fungus in soils that is deposited from bird and bat droppings. It is recommended to wear a particulate mask while raking up or blowing away seed hulls underneath feeders. Many people who contract histoplasmosis don't develop symptoms, but some exhibit mild flu-like symptoms. Rarely, other people can suffer serious complications.

Cryptococcosis is another fungal disease found in the environment, and it also comes from bird droppings. Often associated with pigeon droppings, it is best to wear rubber gloves and a mask when cleaning up scat on feeders and around roosting sites, attics, cupolas and other places where large numbers of birds gather. Like histoplasmosis, many people don't suffer any symptoms. Some just come down with symptoms of a mild flu.

West Nile virus is carried by mosquitoes. Woodpeckers and other birds contract it but don't transfer it to humans, so there is no need to be concerned about getting this disease from your feeders.

Keeping your feeding station clean and refreshing the sites are quick and easy ways to stop the spread of avian disease and other diseases from bird droppings.

A quick dry-clean is recommended each time you refill your feeders. Dump out the old seeds before adding any new and knock out any seed clumps. Also, wipe down the feeder with a dry rag to remove the bird scat before refilling it.

You should wet-clean your feeder if there are obvious signs of mold or mildew. Dead birds near feeders or on them are another indicator that a major wet cleaning is needed. Use a sanitizing solution of one part bleach to nine parts warm water, or purchase a commercial bird feeder cleaning solution.

To remove stuck birdseed, use a scrub brush. Insert a long-handled bottlebrush in tubes, and use an old toothbrush to clean other hard-to-reach places.

Dismantle the feeder as much as possible and scour with your scrub brushes and cleaning solution. Clean inside and out and rinse well with hot water. Allow the feeder to dry thoroughly overnight, or lay the parts out in the sunlight before reassembling and refilling it.

Cleaning around the base of a feeding station is very important. Rake up or blow away old seed hulls on the ground. These will accumulate after a long winter or other extended feeding. Add or refresh any mulch or gravel beneath your feeders.

Finally, remember to wash and rinse birdbaths before refilling them with fresh water.

Protecting Woodpeckers

The U.S. Fish and Wildlife Service estimates there are 10 billion resident and migratory birds breeding in North America annually. By the end of the nesting season, there are about 20 billion birds.

The majority of threats to birds are associated with people. Collisions with building windows are one of the biggest killers. Nearly 100 million birds die each year from flying into windows. During migration through cities, they fly into lit skyscrapers at night. Most small songbirds migrate at night and seem to navigate better in darkness than with artificial light. Businesses in tall buildings are beginning to douse their lights during migration, and this has helped.

Collisions with windows also occur at residences. The reflection of sky and trees in windows and glass doors creates the illusion that the flight path is clear. This causes tragic window strikes at home. To see woodpeckers close-up and protect them, move your feeders to within 3–5 feet of window and door glass. This will prevent the birds from gaining too much speed on takeoff and reduces impact. Move feeders to least 30 feet away from windows to stop collisions due to reflection.

You can also apply ultraviolet (UV) light reflective stickers to glass so woodpeckers can see objects instead of reflections. These stickers are clear and often have the shape of a bird. While we can see through them, the outside reflects UV light, which woodpeckers can see.

Studies show the most effective way to reduce window strikes is to hang ¼-inch-thick metallic streamers from the eaves of your house in front of windows. These streamers block the path of woodpeckers in flight. There are many more ways to reduce window strikes, so be sure to check online for more solutions.

Before the bird feeding industry was established, it was common to put table scraps outside for the birds to eat. Very few people wasted any food, so often it was just stale bread or tidbits of other old food. However, woodpeckers don't accept morsels of this type, and this kind of feeding usually draws critters, such as skunks and raccoons, that are not welcome in backyards. So whether you set out attractive ground feeders or simply place food for woodpeckers on cut tree stumps, it is not recommended to use table leftovers for bird feed.

According to one study, pesticides are responsible for killing an estimated 72 million birds annually. Most of the pesticide use is agricultural, but you can support the efforts to reduce the chemical ingestion fatalities of birds in several ways.

It's easy to help by buying only fruit and vegetables in season. Purchasing only organic fruit and vegetables is another option. Or, you may just decide to go organic in your own garden and backyard. Reducing or eliminating your personal use of pesticides and herbicides will not only make the overall environment safer, but the woodpeckers you love will also eat uncontaminated fruit and insects as they stage near the feeders in your yard.

About the Author

Naturalist, wildlife photographer and writer Stan Tekiela is the author of the popular Backyard Bird Feeding Guides series that includes *Bluebirds*. He has authored more than 165 field guides, nature books, children's books, wildlife audio CDs, puzzles and playing cards, presenting many species of birds, mammals, reptiles, amphibians, trees, wildflowers and cacti in the United States.

With a Bachelor of Science degree in Natural History from the University of Minnesota and as an active professional naturalist for more than 25 years, Stan studies and photographs wildlife throughout the United States and Canada. He has received various national and regional awards for his books and photographs. Also a well-known columnist and radio personality, his syndicated column appears in more than 25 newspapers and his wildlife programs are broadcast on a number of Midwest radio stations. Stan can be followed on Facebook and Twitter. He can be contacted via www.naturesmart.com.